Understudies

for Elliot, Sophia & Phoebe

Anne-Marie Fyfe
Understudies
New and Selected Poems

Seren is the book imprint of
Poetry Wales Press Ltd
57 Nolton Street, Bridgend, Wales, CF31 3AE

www.serenbooks.com
facebook.com/SerenBooks
Twitter: @SerenBooks

First published 2010
Reprinted 2014

ISBN 978-1-85411-520-1

A CIP record for this title is available from the British Library

The publisher works with the financial assistance of
the Welsh Books Council

Cover art: 'Chiswick High Road' by Sonya Vine
www.sonyavine.com

Author website: www.annemariefyfe.com

Printed by the Grosvenor Group (Print Services) Ltd

Contents

New Poems

from *Late Crossing* (1999)

From *Tickets from a Blank Window* (2002)

from *The Ghost Twin* (2005)

New Poems

Synchronicity

Miscounting the vital showstop
on rosined high-wire
the former trapeze artiste surfaces
nightly to a dangling premonition.
In a connecting room
the mynah preens on a clawed perch,
sleeks draggled plumage,
tests his splinted wing
by the hooked-back window
keeping a lidded eye
trained on the fire-escape.
Vertiginously close to the empty
well of light, the great void,
she can scarcely discern
clinical fracture-talk
of underpinnings, the chitter of
clipboard notes. Just beyond,
the slip – misjudged by a fingertip –
oscillates, endless, pointless
                              in dead air.
A cerise tangle, arc, parabola
on the x-axis – scales tipping –
a flashback to her father
carried onto the front porch,
his scarf gusting in the wind
of a Chicago evening.
The flapping deafens, the bird orbits
the somnambulating metropolis
while the whole rickety
dumbshow splinters, collapses.

The Understudy

The doctor works hour after hour
under clock-hands stilled at five.

A painterly suspension of the wrist-joint –
such precision on the block.
                              Perspiring,
the physician plucks shirtcuffs, sallow
moments under the knife,
                              glint of the abyss.

The obituarist, far from the scene
of the crux, sharpens Lakeland pencils.

Elevator doors concertina to a standstill.

Upper chambers of the heart hang
by a daybreak. A limp corvine
in the Camellia House cannot find his mate.

Light bleeds into evening, a blunted razor
rests on a porcelain ledge.

The understudy in the wings
applies Leichner No. 5.

Next-of-kin snaps a clean wishbone.
Sirens clamour for last
                              atonements
in south-side plazas.

Plazas chequered with total strangers
asking for the possibility of a light.

Backlit Days

It all begins again in that familiar town
to a mission-bell soundtrack:
in the pool of a table lamp
a woman knits in black and white
shaping a collar in flashback.

It rushes through 'fifties Wyoming, the taciturn
on horseback,
                barrel-house piano
in a gold-nugget saloon bar, then
a trench-coat silhouette on an agency door,
the backlit days of 'thirties starlets
as flickering desk-calendars shed torn
swirled leaves. No closing credits to speak of.

And still it moves to the fastness of a city,
rain-locked,
                the hissed, near-comatose opening
and shutting of tram doors
                        in subterranean dusk
where one boards and none disembarks,
no subtitles, just torchbeam and whirr,
the continuous whirr;
                    the same woman, old now,
searching for children, a low-wattage bulb
still lit in each stripped, re-let apartment.

The Absolute Stillness of Pictures

You're afraid to go to bed, afraid of rising,
while street cats, indifferent,
stalk the car-lot fence, the poster-littered
sidewalks of dawn.
     A call centre requests
the first and third of your six-digit code.
You give your mother's date of birth,
of death, it's all the same now.
Do those wide stockyard avenues
remember her at all?

Across town, an ethereal quiet.
       Spouses
parking-up at the shut mall have nothing to share.

Traffic signals stuck on amber. You're raking
embers, retrieve the remains of a letter
from Virginia: your mother'd kept the stamp
and a tract from that too-familiar,
door-stepping Bible salesman.

Silent nods in the shuttered store.
       Fog's
kept up for days. Highway's closed.

In the town square, static galleries, the absolute
stillness of pictures, quieter than a hundred libraries,
sadder than bookmarks.
      You wrestle
clammy sheets, try to get over. Now
it's the morning Amtrak and the missing stenographer
from last night's late movie.

Then the unlettered keyboard of a child's typewriter,
dismembered mannequins, the future ghosts
of your wartime parents, young again,
watching you in a Labor Day picnic photo.

Or all of you frozen under awnings
by the circus photographer's flash. Then
store fronts and neons all the way home.

Wake. Bedside lamp. Pick up
a gaudy paperback. Desk light. Heels...

Elevator in the Dark

I exhaust all the *when I get out of here*
mantras, then *ways to slow your breathing…*
Two hours and two minutes now.
It's Labor Day Weekend Friday, concierge
long gone, right now he's ordering fajitas
at Garcia's three blocks away.
I've tried *Press button firmly* but no
guaranteed response in two minutes.
Above, only lift gear, dense cloud,
a night sky. Far below, subway tracks,
graffiti, an underworld; and here between,
an abyss of lift shaft. Two blocks east
the night's firefighters clock in, watch
a pre-recorded ballgame maybe, they're
hoping for a slow-news weekend.
I rework classic chess gambits,
list Confederate generals, just forty-nine
states, forget North Dakota, offer
a makeshift prayer or two under
the low green of backup lights. And conjure
that fourth-grade Bible frontispiece,
the ladder headed heavenward, gleaming,
radiant. It all stretches up, up, aeons
of infatuations, commitments, paychecks.
Ordinary enough things to hanker after
in this jammed late Seattle Friday elevator.

21st Century Blues

Security codes, lilies, death stamps.
How long since you recognised
your chalky complexion
in the compartment windows,
your passport photo reduced
to the thinnest transparency?
Ancestors in heirloom albums
no longer look you in the eye.

Excise officials, armed police, headstones.
Winter Saturdays, riding downtown subway
trains, the endless limp search
for faces, post-dated checks lost in garbage,
numberless one-way travel warrants.
The answer's in the evening crossword.
Observe the concentration of passengers,
all headed the opposite direction.

Homeland, refugees, Marine greatcoats.
A sentence, yes, a long one, but you don't die:
shrapnel & firing parties are mere asphyxiating
dreams you evade with each alarm.
Somewhere they're writing your story,
weaving your history in every public library,
collecting signatures for
a worthless conditional pardon.

Tolls, blown-up crossing points.
And where's that map of Antarctica, tied with
a shoelace, you carried everywhere
until paper folds become crevasses
setting floes adrift in a southern ocean?
But still you ride the driverless trains
as funerals process overhead: the subway's
for eternity, your address book's been deleted.

The Mass of Men

Low-wattage filaments quiver
in the town's cheaper lets.
Tuesday again and motel guests
slide safety chains in Detroit dusk.
Indifferent men with luggage-
on-wheels fumble for key cards.

Late-night downtown trains
– a day's heat boxed in – discharge
the last frayed workers with stuffed
grocery sacks. In erased neighbourhoods
zipcoded children sleepwalk:
side-by-side in the blackness, all of us.

In your walk-up the machine-fitter on third
has reshuffled faces of 10th-grade
first-kisses at summer camp, hears
the beauty of the lilies in his mother's
voice, breaking: his current reality
is weather channel, pizza delivery,
a dry cough on the far side of the partition.

All over town couples in peeled rooms
back to back in the dark, feign slumber.
Scenic calendars have most days circled.
Full, lived lives. Appointments kept.
A tone of placid despair.

The ball game postponed until Thursday.

A woman, somewhere, fires the single shot.

Our Reticent Neighbour

A bakelite telephone rings on the mortuary desk.
Voice recognition kicks in, whirrs awkwardly.

They're tapping doors and shutters tonight
the gas-lit length of our street. By the time
you've pounded stairs, crossed a lobby
insinuated Yales into mortices, they've vanished.

Retread the four flights and try again for sleep,
despite search-beams searing the dark. Despite
unmarked ambulances that trawl the suburbs,
half-trained mastiffs that jangle and snarl.

No one's readying for this night's shift.
Word's out. Declassified resumés are destined
for lock waters. A currency broker wakes
in a Third Street tailors' doorway, coughing.

Lutheran rooming-house occupants
make hasty atonements on discovering
their Gideon Bibles bookmarked at Samuel.
The town ursologist leaves one safety-gate unlatched.

The bakelite instrument's terrible jangle subsides.
But surely that's a normally reticent neighbour
rehearsing his C-sharp-minor mazurkas?

Strings

A day that starts with a skiff-load
of puppets on the Mere, a coat-rack
of Pressburger marionettes
in the parlour, a gold-lettered cabinet
displaying plaster heads
with arched looks
in the municipal clock museum.

The booth-lady at the picturehouse
is a glove, the red-bolero'd
usherette leads you
with her unsteady flashlight pool
to a row where each ticket-holder
bobs up and down
like a staggered pianola arpeggio
wires flickering in the carbide beam
and lets you sink into threadbare plush,
the ache of a day's journey
tugging at the brass eyelets
in your elbows and creaking knees.

Tortoiseshell Clasp

Dejá vu at first sight of the landward side
from long-ago afternoons figuring how
our small town looked to the island children.

Town of closed doors where happy and fraught
alike under harbour-hill eiderdowns
shut out Sunday, seascape, horizon.

On the island at last we ponder
that dollshouse seafrontage
framed now in a porthole picture window
in the lobby of the island's one hotel
where a stiff desk drawer harbours
a century's lost gloves, mostly rights.

Mostly right hands held brow-high once
against the sun's squint to spy out
our long-dreamt granite breakwater:
and an eight-year-old skipping on rocks
with a vanilla Ninety-Nine and a tortoiseshell clasp
her parents bought in the high-gabled city.

Walk-On Parts

That renegade gull is watching for me
to make the first slip: there at the top
of every rusted hand-over-hand ladder,
the same gull – there can only be one –
I saw once yellow-beaking a mangled Coke can
in the Alcatraz exercise-yard or eyeing
my ice-cream, years before, on Skerries
strand. A promenade lamp-post strutter
he shuns breakers, stalks the disused
fish-houses, voracious tongue seeking-out
cellophane, polystyrene chip-trays,
renders the daytime frenetic,
tenebrous, with his clamour, his
flappy fatalist tattoo.
                                        I find myself praying
he'll plummet from a dry-docked
trawler's jib, one fine day, mistake
the Jetfoil's windscreen for wide open space.
Funny. I've never actually seen him
take off. Never known the full heart-stop
of his wingspan. Never once looked head-on
into that lashless, browless, gimlet eye.

Les Parapluies

Twenty to one outside
and he's backing
a stiff umbrella
in its northeasterly
assault.
          This side
of dropletted glazing,
saucers on gingham
rattle, clink, against
a cut-glass marmalade jar.
That side, his bespattered
pinstripe cuffs
conceal town shoes.
A news-wrapped flounder's
upturned fisheyes
glaze
          wide-angled
at a pre-lunch universe.
Soaked Assam leaves
cluster, in lucent
china, denying consolations.
The sheltering skiff
casts the bay's sole
noonday shadow.

Grey Bowl of Heaven

Overcast again: on Detroit assembly lines
they dream of this. Washed-up Maine fishboxes,
others, splintered, from Galicia,
a chessboard from out of nowhere.

A Bostonian's coffin passes the home place
on a tractor's tail-lift. Mourning
headscarves blaze in a dry landscape:
the pattering of graveside novenas.

A ruinous winter for locals. You've
still enough vocabulary to detect
indifference, urgency, this many
sea-leagues out from land.

Fifteen schoolyard infants sing
in their re-learned native tongue;
traitorous waters conceal
keels, masts, Castillian chalices.

Beyond the Flaherty's casement
the upcast grey bowl of heaven:
half doors and tombstones face east
in unrequited expectation of rising noon.

Meteorology

Lifebuoys at dusk are a minor attraction.

Like the flippered volunteers who circle
barnacled keels, dreaming of ingots, cannon-shot.

The reinstated harbourmaster rubs
ladder rust from psoriatic fingers.

An over-quota lamprey slipped tidal waters
yesterday; surfaced mid-channel, a double barb
still snagging its gaped mouth.

Island graves are keeping just above water.

The coastguard's sister places coal
on a front room back-boiler fire set for Sunday.

Ties her headscarf tighter:
he's not breathed a word for years.

An unpeopled sloop drifts in poor visibility,
its absence flecking the radar's luminescence.

Sea beds are rich with miscellanea: a doll's
found voice-box floats, released, to the low horizon.

Postcards to Oregon

An angular figure tracks shapes
on the frost-packed shore. An Etruscan
town plan waiting for tides to turn.

Sunday mornings rich with pilchard sauce.

First morning of October's rental,
ill-matched furnishings, remains of summer's
unexpired lease, front-lot rank
with shot garlic. Inside
a 1950s Frigidaire shudders into life.

I stamp postcards to Oregon and Seattle.

Between clearly articulated lanes and alleys
the angled figure sculpts earthworks,
drinks from a litre Evian bottle.

Third lines are invariably hardest.
I set aside the pen and seek out
an enamel coffee-pot, a means
of lighting gas, a passable cup.

Tarpaulined between runway and fence,
the small planes....

By noon, a new Atlantis at his feet,
this man possessed builds his castle
wilfully close to ebb and flow,
dredges a shin-deep moat
that fills as he digs; perfects
crenellated ramparts, sand drawbridges,
one tall keep, a kelp flag for pennant.

We build against oblivion.

A morning's drafts go in the flip-top bin.

First Heartbreak

It's painting lines of oars in rows
on scutch grass, painting floats,
bargaining with August dusk.
It's my uncle priming tea-house
gables, to dry slow under decades
of tall spruce, branches filtering
sunlight. It's the other uncle
unearthing war-time regulation grey
for a chicken shed, the displaced
circling, scratching in grit, bemused.
From the air there's nothing but ladders
propped against blinding Snowcem.

That July two brothers from the other side
of the mountain – bleached overalls,
blowtorches and a light blue
Ford van – gave our bungalow
two coats of brilliant white, the one
time we'd see Gatsby brightness
this side of the bay. White that's embedded
in a lifetime of wedged windows, tacky
doorjambs, blisters bursting
in a noonday sun. White that's twinned
with melted ice-cream, cream soda,
bags of marshmallows, broken hearts.
And always a pup at the lowest rung
yelping at the sheer improbability.

Dog Days on Main Street

Gerard Francis has seen *Henry* in the comics
fry eggs over-easy on a skillet-hot August sidewalk
like this. Sizzling. A woman idles by the phone box.

Behind her grille Mrs. Bell perforates pension books,
Schubert's *Trout* rilling in her head, her fingertips.
Gerard Francis has nine-and-six in savings.

McFetridges' pumps, a Texaco lubricating can.
Doilies, tan tights and snakebelts on Arthur's counter.
Rosina's, slow cats, bleached boxes of peppermint creams.

Gerard Francis steers us way clear of sweetshops with cats,
wants me to spend his sixpence on younger brother stuff.
American comics or a bamboo fishing net.

Two in a queue now for the red kiosk. Moonan's,
bath crystals, apothecarial chalkiness, gloom.
Under the bridge's keystone, sticklebacks, clear shallows.

Quencher wrappers heaped in fly-clustered mesh bins.
Lynns' dairy ice-cream, the chilling bacon slicer.
then Kinney's, *Local Flesher*, chippolatas, silverside.

Mobile library at the bridge. Antrim County ink smudge
and watchful silence over half-glasses. There's a stranger
at the bus-stop opening and clamping shut her purse.

Now Fyfe's, True Crime, Sylvine watermarks on red.
Gerard Francis wants to buy *Nancy* and *Caspar*,
ten cents each, which comes to more than his sixpence.

The telephone kiosk is vacant: I hold the sprung door wide
for Gerard Francis to lean in and press button B.

It's Like This

On sunsets like these
you're sure there's a bird's nest
in the back-lane hedge
where something is stirring,
certain the wild wallflowers
on the Northern Bank parapet
on Main Street are leaning
away from crumbled pointing
to face west.

          On twilights
like these, through
an open scullery door
someone's rattling
in a cutlery drawer
for a biro to write 'Rhubarb'
and 'June 65', listening
for bicycle tyres on gravel.

And her next-door neighbour
on a first-floor ward is looking out
at the same passive light,
cigarette fingers trembling
from Tuesday's ECT.

Just now there's a still, cold
view from the middle bridge
you've never noticed till this moment:
a chill absence of sunset
on sea-ward bungalow windows.

The Filling Station

It's late and your father's smoking
Player's Navy Cut at the wheel;
he stops for petrol at your grandmother's –
same Esso sign but nothing of the small business
Elizabeth Bishop loved, the sons, a begonia
and comic books; nearer the pallid
despair of Hopper's *Gas, 1940*
in the brooding of roadside woods.

You want to insist, *Drive on, don't*
sit revving, the dead can't hear.
                     You remember
an uncle from Inverness, the hum
of adult talk after the funeral,
egg-and-cress rolls one May Friday.

                     Sure, you could
say nothing
            but you'd hate to see the look
on his face when she doesn't
hurry down the lane, zig-zagging
the flashlight, her black wool coat
thrown over slight shoulders,
as his headlights pick up
the white letters of O-X-O on the red cash tin.

Short Strand

i.m. William Reilly (1885-1936)

It's the street-by-street-wise map,
gazetteer, directory,
                    sudden gift
from a Falls Road flute-player
that starts me off tracing
unapproved roads
                    to the lough's
other side where a songbird
with an orange bill whistles
through backyards, blind alleys,
lock-up garages
                    to my tall grandfather
and forty-eight Moira Street,
a landlocked enclave between
Clyde, Victoria and Thompson.

An automatic's echo
                    from barracks
where his estranged
RIC sergeant father ended up
in Twenty-Two.
                    A Sunday peal
from St. Matthew's (not his
persuasion) though he cajoles their
older ones into keeping up
since she died.
                    A calling-out
from the Yard
where that White Star year's
confetti-rounds
                    troubled him less
than the post-war expulsions
when Cootehill Orange Hall
connections
                    couldn't excuse
a Southern name, a Cavan accent,
a Glens marriage.

Barracks, chapel, shipyard
                              and a bleak
after-school trek for the youngest
by Cromac, Botanic,
Pretoria and Colenso to collect
the morphine
                    he can ill afford
a day without these final weeks.

He maps his last route
high out over Legoniel,
the Seven Mile Straight
Rathkenny, the Sheddings,
Cargan Crossroads
                         to Legegrane
past every lit farmhouse
where she sang *The Blue Hills*
those pregnant wartime nights
to his pure
                 hushed
                         melodeon-playing.

Mount Carmel, Sunday

A cry runs the transverse length
of the buildings. Clean, uncreasing
like a man's handkerchief. The line
of short-stay cabins jolts. Haven
of the isolated, internalised, the bereft.
Family saloons arrive with ginger cordial,
cartons of clotted-cream fudge.
                                        This cry
stalls over Reserved Parking
invades pink kimonos, scalloped matinée
jackets, blackout blinds, pillowcases
stacked on drystore shelves; it billows over
elm, yew and rowan, cleaves awkward
but sure to the weatherboard spire
of a neighbouring hawthorned province.

Ballad of the Corner Café

Nothing was, as it is now, or shall
be again, in the deep Kodacolor skies
of rusting scenic postcard stands.

Double doors, a smoky card school,
lost ormolu chimes, Friars Balsam,
Sailor, leave the sea... spinning,
spinning, then the slow incursions
of analgesia and Last Rites.

In its day the Corner Café's salon
plied chinchilla widows in stilettoes
with coconut ice and mandarins.
In its later Cosy Corner guise
it would slip single Woodbines
to local Harry Limes last seen
cupping a single Swan Vesta
out of the streetlamp's arc.

In his day the demobbed owner
kept a weather eye
on a sprung overdoor bell.
                              Now
the last pegboard's chrome hooks
lie on the faded window display's
'fifties holly-paper; a suffocating
wasp's nest frets in the gusts
from a broken scullery pane;
a white rocking horse shivers in the yard.

Full Dress Rehearsal

The house at the end of the line
        was more in its day than these low
           remnants of redbrick cavity walls,
             stray Rhode Islands roosting,
occasional bronze feathers drifting, drifting....

In the house at the end of the main road
        they're readying for a marzipan
and damson jelly morning,
            spruce dressed,
goose stuffing mixed,
          folios on the piano,
a wishbone waiting to be broken.

          One unmarried aunt
clips a tortoiseshell cluster on black silk,
         gift from a once-promising
new vet whose progressive tone didn't
          invite grandparental warmth.

Gable light picks out
         midnight Episcopalians
arriving on a sprung trap,
        coachlamp wicks smoking kerosene
into the night.
       Mother
         in her once-a-year apron
supervises a temperance fruit punch.

That slate-roof house at the end of the metalled road
    has a homecoming candle on the front porch,
        viridian coffee-pot
warming on the cast-iron plate,
        a child's pony on wheels
in the deadlocked woodshed for the eldest.
      The sky fills with seasonal whispering.
        Snow in Martinstown
holds off for another day.

Erasures

It's the transient hour come round
once more as you open the steep casement
over unpeopled streets,
in this historic Belgian town,
paste-up another day's souvenirs.

You dwell without cease on fellow residents
you've passed on the street, the parts
they might have played; how they remain
occupied reliving strategies, manoeuvring
retrenchments of painted lead Huzzars.

Yesterday you photographed
relentless pre-war rollingstock
at every outskirt siding. Then the cafés
in the town square: apricot *tartes*,
Lièigois, cachous, denials, confetti.

So long ago. Knickerbocker sailor suits,
the Archduke's widow in a lacquered chair,
paper lanterns, streamers, silver cake beads,
your balsawood bi-plane, and the long,
candle-shadowed corridors of the war dead.

Deep in your gaberdine you finger a one-way
ticket, to the small schloss you traced
in Austria's dark clandestine heart –
lost again in a snowstorm's flurry –
sudden blizzard or swirling bauble?

Book of the Dead

An elder groundsman stoops,
tubercular, sweeping a tumult of arid
mulch into a low mound,
strikes a lucifer, holds
for the first small conflagration.

Breath-whistling a parchment waltz,
he'll range date-stamped herbicides
in a lime-washed afternoon pantry.
Straightening, half-glancing, he espies
translucent, blue-veined faces
at a high-barred child's window,
drapes timidly parted in the knowledge
that a surfeit of day can bleach *tapisseries.*

Beyond the copse, a slight decline,
then a family of alabaster stones
each complete with small trumpeting seraph
haloed in the white-wolf moon.

Grim Rehearsal

Another day of flies in the Alpengasthof.
Solid rain the entire week.
Display cabinets, black-veiled dolls,
eyes minuscule fishbowls of pure dumb glass.
The tractor rep at the next table swears
the sewing machine's finished in the East:
his stiff wife predicts the future's in wigmaking.

Another funeral since you left,
radon levels checked monthly now.
A glistening black carapace of umbrellas
breaks up beneath my balcony.
Mourners in outsize weather capes drip
by various routes into the *Parking Garage*.
So Schladming. So like a wet week
in Achill, my father buying postcards
and green Republic stamps, scooping
small change from a glass-topped counter,
the owner rushing to pull shopblinds
as the Raffertys' hearse murmurs into the street.

Which train will you be catching? Do
check the high mountain pass isn't cut off
like before. Last night's flies have died, the new
arrivals are digging-in for the long stay,
one of them surrendered untimely
in the bedside water jug. Small wonder
I've not slept a wink in months.

My Alias Returns a Book

Lorca's fastidious seamstresses stalk
aisles with blunt shears, excise smudges,
fingerprints, small scintillas of doubt.
Edgar Allan Poe's caped gendarme
clatters on an iron roofwalk. So it goes.
Let inquiries begin once unrepentant
librarians have been sequestrated.
Interrogate doppelgängers in quiet rooms
across state boundaries. Witness
reconstructions of old Perry Masons.
Permit yourself to disregard motive
as O. Henry scoops cake crumbs with
a letter opener in the Reader's Digest lobby.
Labyrinthine tales in the Tower of Crime.

In bookless hinterlands a moon climbs
over parking lots outside the library's
high shuttered windows and doors.
Someone needs to identify shelf gaps,
absent alliterative titles, put out alerts
for the unransomed: those bundled in
a roadster's trunk; some incognito amid
toothpicks, or under motel beds;
a lurid few that hover jacketless
in the decommissioned shuttle over
Nevada. The wise sleuth will mistrust
alibis, cross-examine closing statements.

Marlowe by desklight's the only known
antidote for conspiring stenographers.
Don't forget to earmark that Hart Crane
preface, underscore a final paragraph by Melville.
Finely annotate Miss Dickinson's Swiss
and precisely unpunctuated exclamations.
Heft each of them page for page
as forensics in raincoats check returns
for eczema flakes, dried saliva, matching
evidential specks on a slew of mildewed
National Geographics when Chandler steps
into Act 3 with a revolver. Suddenly.

Taking the Red Bus Home

for Elliot Robilliard at six months...

Elliot's at home here in this sashaying
uptown riverrun *Love-me-Like-a-Rock* world
of packed Japanese students, offstepping
trainee estate-agents, homebound
earlyshift Firestone operatives.

Here in a lie-back pushchair. Here.

Elliot's at ease where he can harmonize,
drift, babble – to rhythms, swerves,
sleeping policemen, lights on amber,
the sharp pullaway – stop after request stop.
Always someone boarding: someone
strutting purposefully away
in the cinematographic ebb and flow.

The 94 has unmapped upper reaches
beyond the dreams of pushchair users.

But Elliot's at-home-est on the newest,
bendy, all one level, tossed together
on stormy, one-way, stop-start trade-routes
all the way to the city's westward ridges,
all the way home, past the end of Hollies Road,
the request bell ting-tinging still
in the all-nighter dreamtime remix
of sirens, priceless small-talk, diesel revs,
grasshopper fussings of inaudible iPods,
the swish open-shut sigh of pneumatic doors.

The Painted Smile

When exactly the day of liberty
dawned she hardly knew despite
reflection, musings, half-sick
of shadows: was it some
passing gallant and his convoy,
captive of a mere glance? Or was it
when the mirror cracked?

The rest was more or less foretold,
borne by water, in the beauty
of stateroom lilies, pennanted prow
passing first houses, her delicate frame
escorted with Christian chivalry to where
they crossed themselves amazed to see her
brought into their far, flag-hung city.

She'd withstood vacant stares too long –
centuries, it seemed – that cavalcade
of trinket sellers, pontificators, diplomats
crowding her low-lit corner
of a four-grey-walled riverbank keep,
their dreams brought to her
doorstep, to lie there. Die there....

And now, presented to him at last
(and his Oleg Cassini-gownéd lady)
the war hero whose gaze once –
past non-reflective glass and tasselled ropes –
first broke the spell, would he still muse
upon that captured look or see her *just
a cold and lonely lovely work of art?*

Ghost Writer

Check his papers for the fuller story:
announcements, lettings, obituaries.
Mondays startle in green ball-point.
Trace years through loose-leafs, Woolworth's
spirals, marbled hardbacks. Pick out
nights he'd write without lamps. Awkward,
vaguely looped jottings, often after absences,
then a sudden cold front, blocked days.
In ruled margins, hints of liaisons,
apartments, telephone prefixes. Tricky,
isolating dreams from the actual. Sundays
give clues: erratic press-dried crumbs,
coffee-rings, a butter smear, seals
of the authentic life. Lately, losing names,
crossing out, overwriting. Few efforts
at explication. Back then he'd constructed codes
(diffident, wary), used pictograms, even thumb
sketches, black, white and hatching, the whole
spectrum. Just don't query them now.

A Good Trade

He's long gone now, gone to ground they say,
the tradesman who sharpened the crescent's
blades, scythes, scissors. He'd arrive
each spring, park next the pillarbox
and collect his day's worth.
                              Last time
he huddled in sheeting rain, a Sunday, oddly,
recounting troubles, family stuff, how he'd never
have dreamt of asking, would honour the debt
surely, within days, a week at the outside.

Last Tuesday, before waking, I saw him
by our rusted gate, tan shopcoat, seams
greased with age, notebook and blunt pencil
in a high pocket, life in a regulation kit-bag,
telling my son it was good to be back
here with us, for good,
                              after that other business.

Half-saluting at me down our hallway
he launched into talk of politics,
how Yeats — that great house too,
its picket fence and door pull,
had been on his ledger once —
how the poet had so misjudged
such trades as his.
                              I couldn't shake them off
all morning, the two of them, poet and grinder,
the whetstone dropping slow now, both lying
down where all the treadles start,
                              old themes
of long embittered hearts. The kitchen scissors
won't cut parsley, the bread knife that sliced
clean through our thirty years lacks its old edge.

Late Crossing (1999)

No Jitterbugging in the Aisles, Please!

We'd take them one by one,
chairs from emptied rooms,
to the park at our road's end.
We'd set them out in rows,
wait for the shuffling
guests who don't appear.

I'd put RESERVED
on the front two rows,
slip you last requests
while you'd hitch your too-slack suit,
ad lib a final solo
on that first silver sax again
till the shudder of the early
subway trains past the park
would signal day
and we'd head together,
your sax-case and my one
chair, to the station,
leaving behind flattened
grass, the scatter
of cloakroom tickets.

Friday

It was a summer-wet city evening in the patio-garden;
leaves were glossy with rain in the last of a reddened
light. She liked to watch him in shadow, sitting to one
side of the open french doors; she liked the way he held
a beer, the way he packed his pipe, pressing down firm-
ly with his forefinger, just like her uncle used to do.
Should she tell him now, or later, or not at all. *We must
cut back the fire-thorn*, he said, a voice startling the silence.
She fingered the silkiness of her yellow dress, worn
tonight for the first time. She had moved her lips to
speak when the phone rang, rang again, rang insistently.
Their eyes met for just an instant as she rose from her
chair and moved towards the voice in the next room.

Motel

Here in this sweltered suburb
the call of an owl disquiets
and for a moment I'm that child
who believes in the banshee.
I draw the dampened sheet closer,
push my foot across to feel
for yours – but waken alone:
a woman in a late-night movie
screams through the wall; over the way
there's the faintest of opera;
and still an owl is calling:
the irrefutable wail
of a mother for a lost child.

Broken Journey

Cruising down the freeway
on an interstate long-haul
he lost his place
for a moment;
stared blankly
at an unfamiliar landscape,
a lunchbox, magazines,
a pair of hands on the wheel.

Dropping a gear instinctively
he swerved off
into a truck-stop
at the precise second
when the shutter lifted
and he was back
firmly in the picture.
He limped towards the diner
reassured by his reflection
in the plate-glass front.
He remembered his mother
unable to find the kitchen;
she had ended her days
in a family of strangers.
But he was only forty.

He ordered strong coffee
and dialled his woman;
his heart lurched and steadied
when he heard her voice.
He told her he'd be
in time for supper,
asked about the kids.
Picking up a burger
he hit the road again
nervously, looking out
for the right exit sign.

Interstate

Half-eaten fries, the remains of hash browns,
fill the table's distance between them.
She scoops the car keys, says she'll not be long.

In the washroom mirror she checks her face
close up; sees years of wearied waiting.
She steps into a sticky afternoon.

How long before he'll notice, before he'll ask –
the forecourt is nauseous with diesel and ocean –
ask if anyone's seen a woman in middle years.

She's onto the freeway, jittering across lanes.
And why, he'll wonder, now that the kids are gone,
now that they're free to hit the road each spring?

She overtakes on automatic, clearing Carolina –
recalls the one dream he has left, of building a boat;
upriver in summer; dry-dock in winter. The two of them.

An unforeseen calm settles with sundown: she longs
for nightfall on unbroken stretches of highway.
It's clear ahead as far as her eyes can see.

Home

In the dream I'm in a
white house by the bay

watching a funeral pass;
a woman in black chiffon

sits high in the second car.
I cry out, she stares ahead.

I drop the silent telephone
and shuffle through dead letters

in the hall: reading the names
I open the outer door

to the sound of lake water
and walk among ornamental trees

on an island adrift
in a tranquil sea.

Cushendall, 1959

Looking back to that Sunday
after a day on the mountain
pulling and plaiting rushes

I see her in a rose-print frock
slicing lettuce and hard-boiled eggs
while we wait on the front lawn

in the breeze coming off the sea:
the starched frock rustling
like dried paper as she brushed

in and out from the scullery
and I catch even yet
a hint of her Blue Grass scent.

The Orchard

My only grandmother had waist-long hair
tight in a bun in the daytime, wore black
for the husband and son she'd lost. Brown
hessian covered her piano. She never
mended the tied-up swing in the orchard.

But her bantam's eggs had whin-coloured yolks
and she griddled farls in the afternoon
to the tune of *Mrs Dale's Diary* as I'd listen
and watch her floured hands from the window-seat.
Fasting from midnight and smelling of Pears',
we'd take the Volkswagen to early Mass.
In the gas-mantle-hiss of an evening, to a tall
clock's tick and the occasional hum
of a motor on the nearby Ballymena line,
I'd read the book she bought for my holiday,
thinking I'd never heard of a sadder thing
than the scarecrow that longed to be liked.

I never saw my grandmother's piano
without its cover, never got to play
in the orchard.

Backyard

A bird with feathers of blue
Is waiting for you
Back in your own backyard.
                    – Billie Holiday

They were picking tar with a stick
from their new plastic sandals
when they caught sight of it caught
in a flapping shirt on the clothesline
– bluer than any blue they knew.

OK, their mother said, there was room
on top of the old radiogram.
Next day she brought back from town
a cage with a mirror and bell
and a blue bumper packet of Trill.

Word wasn't long getting out:
when Mrs McNeill came from Cedar Avenue
to claim her missing Zoë
she brought them a green bird instead
to show them, she said, her gratitude.

The new green bird wasn't much interested
in those children; wasn't bothered
by any reflection in a mirror; didn't even
sing, it seemed, in the same key.
But there was still picking tar with a stick.

Late Crossing

Past Carlisle
and a hundred dead
to the night boat
I chase vanishing
tail-lights through
relentless drizzle
and listen for news
of visibility in Malin.

Soon I will stand in
the teeth of a Gale Eight
on the *Ailsa's* deck
as morning berths
just out of reach
on an unseen coast
where a sole harbour lamp
signals an end to
the longest night.

New Year Departures

The parting was always a wrench:
standing to one side of the lane,
your worn, brown V-neck pulled over
pyjamas for warmth; you'd shrug
and we'd wonder if this...
if this was to be the last.

I'd reverse the lane's length,
pause on the corner – how small
you'd look in that moment, head high,
smile holding – a last glimpse, then
to Larne for the morning ferry:
conditions unfailingly bitter.

I'd picture you on every dip
and swell of those twenty-two sea-miles,
would see you in the kitchen....
Would you watch the January bluster
from the back door, think only
of winds, high seas, stormy crossings?

Last Things

I take your things
in a tagged plastic bag
across the resounding lino –
the car keys and wallet,
your grey tweed jacket,
its smell of tobacco –
and pick up your car
from the empty park.
Don't choke, you'd say,
it should start first time,
your voice in my head
as clear as the ringing
of the evening Angelus.

Number Nine

In my father's house
you could hear the sea
in every room,
see Scotland
on a clear day
from the garden.
The morning we buried him
there was a note in the hall
in his well-formed hand:
BACK IN FIVE MINUTES.
No-one wound
the clock that night.

The new people
in my father's house
have soundproof double-glazing
and windows in the roof
but I still see him
hunkering on the step
on a good day
with the first cigarette
or tuning in for
the late forecast,
half-awake to the sound
of waves.

Birds, Martinstown

It was a feature of that July.
Small towns of them congregated
on aerials, telegraph wires –
humdrum lines on a beaten sky.

She took it for a sign,
not just the summer's failing
but of tension in the wires.
She woke each day in a sweat

as random numbers of magpies
swooped aimlessly into view –
her mother would have kept count,
however long, till they evened.

On the day the downpour eased
he caught her look at Happy Hour.
Each waited for the other to let go.
She remembered there was still August.

Interior

Charleston Farmhouse, Sussex

Last burst of Indian summer
seeps from the pastel-wet orchard;
we find these rooms chill in the shade.

I take in the gentian sky,
red chimneys, a samphire on ridge tiles
from the library's half-open window.

For a trace of a second your fingertip
sparks with the silk of my blouse
and the afternoon misses a beat.

No longer do the thin wooden beds
under light-faded Omega prints
recall only the cold and the dead.

I discuss with the tour guide a gouache
of the church at Cassis, you flick
the pages of an *À la Recherche...*

No Far Shore

It will be winter when I untie
the boat for the last time:
when I double-lock the back door
on an empty house,
go barefoot through bramble
and briar, measure each
stone step to the slip.

It will be night-time when I row
to the horizon,
steady in North-Star light
the darkened house at my back.

It will be winter when I draw
each oar from the water,
shiver,
and bite the cold from my lip.

Tickets from a Blank Window (2002)

Late Caller

The woman on the other end
says she's my sister, long lost.

I want to believe but I've lived
too long in the certainty
of no such sibling. Prove it.
Have you slate-blue eyes? Do you
sing? All the women in my family sing.
We have voices like honey.
Do you take night trains? Eat dates?
Fear rivers? And don't suffer fools?
And where the hell were you for the third
decade of the family rosary or
when I wanted a sister to share
late-night dance-hall secrets,
or needed a bridesmaid –
a godparent for my firstborn?

Hang up. Press dial-back. My sister
has withheld her number. Didn't say
if she was younger, older, a twin.
It might have made a difference.

Wrong Side of the Moon

Since the night he was never found
his mother wonders what it's like for him,
wrong side of the moon, in a rust-riddled
seaplane, the mission easier this time,

no take-off or landing drill, no air-mail
letter home, or tension over cyclones,
electric storms: nothing now
between him and desert stars that move

further as he nears. Must keep alert,
steer clear of the sleep that beckons
in this sky of near misses. On quiet nights
he hums *South of the Border*, snatches

of *Valencia*, plays the odd game
of gin rummy in his head, filling time
until the dawn that's always on the rise.
He longs for the glow of a just-lit Woodbine,

to skim the forestries of childhood,
hear her whisper, her heart against flight,
Over – my – dead – body –
not once, but over and over again.

6, Sloop Lane

In a night air thick with low tide
and shadows of long-ago children
I trace that holiday-let among blind
alleys stepped up from the harbour.

I want you to know that the house
is smaller than I remember
an ill-fitted screen door and withered
Chronicles, a flat tube of glue
among flies on a teak windowshelf.

Promenade hotels echo too few residents.

But you'd still know the out-of-hours dentist's
close by on the hill where I fretted with an abscess,
the gents' outfitters where we found
the stormcoat that never quite fitted.

I want to tell you every last
tang-laden, mast-clinking bit of it
but even if I could mail you
or waken the dead call-collect
you'd want to know what
in this world I was talking about.

Marriage Lines

In the dogday of a foundling summer
I sift baptismal ledgers, standing
in need of a turning point, a trail
to the tall untalked-about grandfather
whose mid-afternoon grew dark
with the slow losing of the girl
in eyeletted boots. Their elopement had coincided
with the Rising: irreparable sunderings.

The Virginia road is borderline,
a montbretia-blazed funeral crawl behind balers
in a gustless sky-cleansing downpour.
Nothing between copperplate lines;
the churchyards keep none of his brothers.
A country of roadside blackspot-grottoes,
early-closings and rock-hard sweets in clouded jars.
Roadsides that have the cure
for everything but the heart.

Tickets from a Blank Window

Last night at last I caught the train
to Summertown, eight thirty-five,
I took a ticket from a blank window.
The tannoy coughed a small delay.
And then. A route I feel I know.
The city draws away from me:
I stare into the backs of lives
still living out in lighted rooms where
stories flick and go.
                            No sleeping car,
I settle in my winter coat and
watch the window-woman's face. What
changes will you see when I step down?

So many times I've thought about
your waiting there, mornings when the guard
would catch the mail and raise his flag
and you would walk away.

First Houses

On bright cold-war afternoons
before I started Mill Street School
my mother taught me the perfect lip
and curve of a cup and saucer –
then a solid, angled house
with endwalls and sloping gable:
I'd add the tied-back curtains,
front door with a seven,
borders of big-leaf flowers
crayoned neatly to the line.

When I wanted to know if her mother
had taught her to do house numbers
she told me about the illness,
about going away to her grandfather's,
not seeing her mother again.

I soon forgot to include the curl
of chimney smoke, my eaves
went wobbly, shutters less straight,
the seven barely readable.
I stopped drawing perfect homes.
For nice families.
Even before my mother got sick.

Vacant Possession

The spirits of our first real house hung
in years of embossed floral patterns
under layers of flaky wartime distemper.
It wasn't ceiling damp, the wasp-riddled attic,
the labrador decomposing in a stair-carpet
among shallow lupins. It was rooms that would never
be aired of dying and sniping. The summer
couldn't reach corners. Houseplants yellowed.

Tiffany lamps, a dresser, stripped doors
did little to lift the chill. Our children's
jokes rang in cupboards, hallways, landings.
They complained of a cold underfoot.
Vague histories savaged our night-dreams, days
we woke to a solemn inertia; birdsong
rarely graced our end of the street.
The morning we left, the spirits rumbled,
rattled windows. Razed
the garden shed like a playing-card house,
irked, in the end, at our lack of staying.

Our House

I come home late to find
my key won't turn in the lock.
Murmurs drift from rooms.
Through the letterbox a child's bike,
a woman's coat on the banister. Beige.
No one answers our door
its scarlet gloss dull now.
I walk up my neighbour's path,
relief as she opens her door.
But she shifts when I say
I'm from next door. No. Some mistake.
The next-doors are long gone,
no word if they'll ever be back.
People inside? No. Never.
She's not heard a pin drop behind
those walls.
        When I get back
to our red door they're switching
off lamps, climbing stairs.
Our bedroom is the last to go.

L'Air du Temps

It overtakes as he hurries to board
flight 872 from O'Hare
to JFK on a shirt-collar damp
evening, a scent he can't start
to describe. Words like dragonflies flit
in his mind. He registers the backs
of women of the incoming flight,
sure she's here – within reach –
and he has only to find her. He quits
his line and trails walkways and newsstands,
escalators, even the chilled chapel,
catches – like an old tracker dog –
new luggage, old sweat, stale cigar-ends,
on the edge of nausea as each new woman's
scent rattles him further.
It's all he's had of her all these years
and he doesn't begin to know
its name. He finds himself in the duty-free
parfumerie: a crisp, maquillaged
assistant proffers him testers.
Chanel perhaps...? That clear summer...
and now this last chance, but the headiness
of the moment's sensation is slipping.
He tries to hold on like he's holding back
the years in the sharp passages between
nostrils and brain. *Je Reviens?*
she says, *or Rive Gauche.* From a distance –
then from a more distant distance –
from a much longer way off –
A glass of water, maybe? – her breath
too close to his own, closing in,
at the precise second 872
is lifted clean out of the clouds
and fragments into a dazzling
blue and uncluttered expanse.

Passing Through Rooms at Eventide

They resume each night in the balm of aniseed:
wedding-album poses under disconnected
room-lights, make small-talk in Amish
shirt-collars, play Persian Roulette with blanks,
turnabout, blindfold for that 100% frisson
as the wireless submerges between wave-lengths.
He thumbs a nightly gazetteer that was once
her uncle's; she pats another day's undone
needlepoint, ochre-yellow skeins oily
from overfingering. Step-for-step they prowl
the apartment's temperate regions
checking for drippy faucets; he plays,
in passing, arpeggios on a hall-cold upright.
Relentless, she readies clocks, rewinds,
sets each to a different time-frame
and sashays like a girl who waits to be kissed.
A girl who wants to be kissed. Properly.

Winterwood

Through treble-thick stone converted
stable walls I hear a horse canter in puddles
– close-up – bidden slow
at temporary lights on the cobbled way.
Night-bus headlamps sweep drystone
walling. Stark with no passengers
to speak of. A relief driver focuses hard
on the hill-edge poplar windbreak;
awaits the blur of amber; glances
night-skyward, tense with unpredictable hemispheres,
the aligning of planets. And you reach out to me
in the sealed dark of our windowless world,
have me stroke the back of your neck
as I emerge from companies of village ghosts
that follow and find me, far from home
on a street where I've never been,
alighting perhaps from a lit bus that slowed
but never stopped. We slip soundly,
waken to coachouse quiet and the hush of crows.

Late in the Evening

She doesn't say much in the weeks after
admission: voices from before
disfigure vacuous evenings
as visitors reverse darkwards,
catching by the main gates a fox's
listless fear. Abandoned, she observes
how she sidesteps to Geraldo full-on,
on a hairsbreadth station, submerging
random echoes of missed loves, scratching
images of undreamt babies; turns
her head towards her only child's muffles
from miles off
                or from a star-lit sycamore
brushing the night-secure fire-escape
by her room at the eaves of the world.

One of Those

Eighteen at one count. Every stray in the townland.
But she'd only, she'd say, have four in the kitchen.
The needy. The same fare, though, as the outside cases.
Coddled yolks and a half tin of this month's offer.

The other thing started on the phone somewhere
behind her left ear, she said, a tinny ticking
like a radiator left to cool. *Tinnitus,*
she'd say, when asked, *or one of those.*

Stopped taking the papers. Couldn't fit words to find clues.
Downs dizzier than acrosses. Cats grew sluggish
as the hatchback stagnated on gravel, parcel-shelf
catching the noon nicely low, taking three cats at a stretch.

No one saw her slide the grocery boxes from the porch.
She unplugged the extension, no longer answered the knocker.

They snaggled over her eiderdown, watched
by a Saint Theresa with broken plaster hands. Even
outsiders, the feral, were slipped in, stealthed round her coma
for days. Then one by one, ravening, moved off into the trees.

Afternoon on Central Plains Avenue

In the suburbs of the lamented it is always late. Rumour
is rife. None has forgotten the rattle of loam on a lid.

Smiles are the order of the day – the week – and neighbours
are hardly at home in the dilapidations of rented rooms.
Phones go unanswered and cat-flaps are sealed.
                                                    Cleaned
uncollected milk bottles clutter the stoops. Meat safes
are close to high.
                        Singing is rare. Gloves shift
but swimsuits stay on shelves and no-one fears heights.

In the country where snow is general and the undertaker
is king, the only books on loan are elegiac.
Fines are exempted.
                        There is only
one season and just enough light to grow bluebells.

Occasionally someone recalls the headiness
of apple peelings and shutters are locked.
                                                Churchyards
are of the past. Cloud density eclipses the sun
                                            moon and stars.

Uniforms of Snow

Full heads pick up gravestones, railings,
as I leave town for another
bedside night of her troubled
breathing... and think of him in there
long-buried and waiting.

He'll have known for weeks now,
have sensed the willing hesitancy,
known she'll make it in the end,
sons and grandsons carrying her
the last measured journey.

I flick small hurried rainspots
from the windscreen, pursue
a snaking recent skid-line
for half a mile or more, alive
to the nearness of ditches and death.

That frost-packed length of earth
– unbroken half of the double-plot –
will take some shifting: he'd be keen
to see her settled before snow,
before December tightens its grip.

Morning on Bridge Street

This new address is lighter than airmail:
on blue my street name looks faint, watered.
I unwrap my mother's fine-bone chattels,
sugar bowl crazy with hairline fissures.
In 5 a.m. still, the locals aver
that time hangs slow, conscious of being
a stone's throw from the not-long dead
who thrive on such broken mornings. The blind
accordion-player on the bridge hollers
it's the real, the absolute, time of day.
Thanks you for the chink of currency.
Passers-by strain to catch his underplayed
wheeze. The postman abandons his route
in small hours. Residents
listen out for a noiseless whistle.

Chartreuse

The woman at the corner of Sunset
and Main in the dilute green of evening
is wearing my mother's face.
                              I shadow,
in determined steps, feet that make no
mark on rain-wet paving – follow
but can't close – stalling over gaps
between slabs from habits of caution,
dragging my hold-all of unrhyming
cadences and broken glassware.
                              She pauses
at a black-edged postcard in the hardware
window, quizzes diffident strangers
about a lost rosary, the whereabouts
of motherless infants, shifts through
ill-lit laneways as shopfronts dissolve,
whole streetfuls of them.
                              I search
the night-long map for a woman
wearing my mother's face. Her face.

The Ghost Twin (2005)

The Ghost Twin

The urge for headway, to make that
last-chance gas station before closing,
the last-minute-cancelled single room.

And then the short-lived standstill.

Shallow sleep at best, a jolt
every forty minutes to red digits
that seem to count backwards.

On your corridor all doors have
even numbers and chains.
                        You
wonder if this one has ever
witnessed the lone last struggle
at four, the long zipped bag
at daybreak.
              On the veneer night table
headed notelets curl under a phone;
no one has thoughts to share.

An unframed overdesk mirror
gives you the hazed
penumbra of the ghost-twin.

In lower-ground kitchens the night
porter cracks seventy-two eggs for
breakfast.
            You wrestle solutions to
the impossible clue in the top corner
of an abandoned acrostic you'd still
not complete even if you had five
of the seven letters that spell cortège.

Hour of Stone

The Baptist clockmaker in the Corner House
rouses, sensing inexact amplitudes. Out-of-true
sugar-tongs chink in temperance hostelry basins.

Night is a baleful mystery. Moon
skirts eerie round edges, follows
the winding stair, chamber after lowering chamber.

Beyond, tide eddies in anticipation. Corbies swoop
on mullions against red-moon clouds. Far below
a dislocation of rough consonants rises up.

Singing. Clacketting heels on wool-yard stones
herald the last housemaid's appearance on Rose Street.
Watery Judas-kisses snuffle her elegant ankles.

Curaçao Dusk

A plane flies off a map's edge
today. At the console, O'Hara inhales
the ozone of Curaçao dusk.
Manilla postcards, weightless with
preprinted greetings, flutter in confined
space, franked, illegibly signed.
The manifest's well under payload.
Faces in cabin windows are graven,
waxy masks, their sightlines
uninterrupted by pitchy flights
of eastbound ebony swans.
The hold's a chaos of tethered
cockatiels, small gods from Surinam.
Bursting valises disgorge wrist-watches,
standby parachutes, a crushed trumpeter's
mute. The co-pilot stows
isobar charts, taps the compass
twice for luck: he mouths a childhood
formula under clearwater skies
before resuming routine announcements
to the remnants of a cabin crew.

Magyar Post

Fifth frontier, twenty-two hours
from Ostend, custom queues under arclights.
An intermitting blue road slithers off the grid.

Each July – my father smoking too hard,
my mother heart-still – I'd concentrate on
stamp-collection pages, or cradle
the department store doll with T-bar shoes
(schoolyard rumour of shedfuls of impounded
toys…) Then the slow build-up in second,
holsters shrinking in the car's rear window.

Signal, mirror, ignition: one military
strobe-striated bridge and we're through
to a country where thunder pummels
unlined windows our whole first night.

Rainfall and lurid dreams. Vast
cellophanes of on-approvals – kingfishers,
red-capillaried butterflies, olympians
cutting overarm through pools –
scatter unhinged off squared
loose-leaves. I wake to the absolution
of afterstorm, and day-long disquiet
until we find the shut kiosk,
cornice pocked since fifty-six,
grille window lined with limited editions.

Novgorod Sidings

Virtual snow on the line, a starry
damask night, the train quits
the virtual station. Wellwishers
gather on the cinderpath, not knowing

how to say goodbye. Passengers
with tall hats in half windows alight
in the opening pages. A red signal
power-cut lasts an entire chapter.

But the couple ring true; emerge from
lost strands. There is grey in her hair
now, cologne hangs in the lull
of stale compartments. Destination

their long-shut summer-house. He carries
her portmanteau in one hand, an octave
mandola in the other. No need
of words. Luggage racks cleared

supper-car mantles cooling. Unlit
factories, grain-stores, mosques dissolve
in the filters of darkness, past telegraph
poles, a lone traveller on a snow-stormed

bridge, isolated railroad hostels.
He notices she's lost an earring, one freshwater
pearl. A running motif. The rest is non-
linear and poorly focused. The engine

slows at the first tunnel, erases carriage
after relentless carriage from the frame.

The Events of May

The ambulance depot windows blaze
in the surveillance of hills.
                              Fullbeams
morse through trees on the pass.
                              Still
in this quarter men feign helplessness.

At no. 47 a stalled couple hope for Friday
like the wait for the end of history.

Steamed and resealed bills gather
dust on the meterbox; a blue-
and-red-edged envelope is losing
its *Luftpost* sticker to mice.
                              Nothing
arrives, nothing is sent on. At night
the couple windowshop for eternity.

She settles on three rubies.
                              A widow
in ground-floor rooms listens
at party walls; hoarder of news-cuttings
and red salmon, she dusts the payphone
in the hall overlong.
                              Stair-treads
day and night.
                    Hotel doormen track
the late operator, the random gatherers.

In 32 a lone boy plays a pre-war
Bechstein too fast.
                    On street corners
funerals keep passing and re-passing.

Sans Souci's eglantine borders
are spreading out of control.

Shooting on the Street

A Saturday for wedding shoes.
Last item on the list. Strappy, open,
not too dance-hall high. A Grandstand
slow-printer of a day: my father
in our sitting-room at home will be
zoning in on recurring laps of a circuit
concentration effortless behind
curtains that shut out the margin
of coastal light. Slight late-morning talk
by the sub-post-office as I wait
for the downtown bus. Car exhausts,
electric floats. Condensed tarmac
morning. The greengrocer arranges
button mushrooms, winter kale:
when I get back on an afternoon
91, he will be not-long-dead.

I step down, shoes in a chainstore bag.
I'd said yes to the box. Tentative. And
to keep them in after. My father by now
will be steadying the vertical hold
for a ten-to-six local news bulletin.

Central Time

We board the six-o-five together
after a three-day layover. My mother
has to know if it's the *Atcheson, Topeka and
the Santa Fe*. And she's that girl again
under the projector's lightbeam, scarlet
lipstick in monochrome grandeur,
sweeping stairs, a charred ruin;
then someone walking you home.

Tonight, Central Time, anxiety or overt
terror. No idea where she's headed.
I settle her in the dining car, offer
the brief amnesias of hot coffee. She
whispers the car-steward smokes
like a young Clark Gable. Iron squeals
and hisses the night long, steam
whistles at long-gone crossings, whole
counties of cactus and storefront towns vanish.

In the hotel cab I expand on parting
and sorrow. She's thinner than
I'll ever remember. A noncommittal
clerk who's seen too many shifts
scrutinises her bags, rings a desk-bell.
She clutches a life in Kodachromes
in the fat handbag with the butterfly clasp,
gives me her wedding ring for safe-keeping
as she faces the narrow stairs
with her wooden-fobbed roomkey.

No. 23 from the Eastbound Platform

She's there in a dust-sheeted room
hair tied back (in my cotton smock!)
glossing a magnolia door at dusk:
a child in a number eight shirt
ricochets his ball off that gable –
the one with the fatal flaw –
a lithe collie snipping at his heels
as he dreams of a Spurs trial.

I'm winded with the ache for this house
we never took: jolted grace-nights
of District Line reckonings, *voltes-*
faces between exchange and completion.
We'd signed, measured windows
saw ourselves rise mornings without number
to tog-out schoolgoing children
swap tense morning signals under radio talk
scrape laminate windscreen frost.

The Upminster 6:10 halts. French
door handles rattle. Stepping into
the front carriage I feel the lurch
back, then forward to nowness
to sills of peeling neglect
ivy-sagged splintering trellises...
The woman in the house lets
us depart, sets her brush on a tin's edge.

Waterloo and City

The underground today is a transit of rooks
packing-out seats, arm-rests, staking each
inch of platform: who outstare, opaque
into catacombs of limed tunnelwork, monitor
reflections of frenetic wingspan in cracked panes.

A compartment-quiet tactile as the crypt;
perhaps an inaudible echo from kindred lines,
the torpor of wheel grinding track, station
by static station, the oddly strangulated
whistlestop at randomised light changes.
By eleven-ten the northern network is choking
with black plumes and melancholy. Cacophonies
of mynahs mimic tannoy bulletins. Drivers
on premium time rev in sheds, wait in neutral –
cellared darks electric with tacit awareness.

Retreat

The dacha tilts incautiously these days, the gash
more raw than before. Myopic
windows gaze on the morning's jet-stream.

Suitcases of tinsel and lights slither to attic-eaves.
A dismantled cot slumps against mattresses
as dresser crockery huddles to starboard.

Cars slow fender-tight, occupants meet
on fissured clay to examine impacted roots,
torn play-den clutter exposed, embarrassed....

A chimney-cowl crashes on the patio, red
earth tiles follow. South-facing shutters dangle
fearful, indolent, towards an emptying fishpond.

Pigeon Coup

Mornings I hear them warble through Venetian
scarves in my wardrobe, laddering shantung,
scattering allergic feathers in their wake.
I'm used to fatal thuds stunning the glass
as I shower, to finding the less streetwise
still warm, dead in suds at my toes.
And a frontstep confettied with spatterings
of vermin-department subpoenas
as burgeoning windowpane cohorts
lay waste to my artichoke beds.

Intelligence hasn't filtered through yet
of lint-cossetted family biscuit tins
where I salvaged wing-shattered seabirds
till the clouds would have them back –
for the most part.
                    I've lost count of pathologies;
and of crossed ice-lolly-stick headstones.

Today I face – dry-throated – a bullet-head
ringtail trashing the pillow, his
monocular gaze judgemental.
He shifts from one scaly leg to another
febrile talons redder than iron-hot red.

Cirque Des Illusions

The Slovak troupe arrives well short
of a moonsharp midnight:
they tally my crumpled collection
of sequenced Bazooka Joe wrappers.
One spit and I'm in. Overlooking
pyjama-cuffs under a belted
Saint Louis' blue gaberdine.

Mr Novacek, funambulist and plate-thrower
in an old war-coat, and Freya,
world's smallest bird-woman,
bump wordlessly beside me
in the cycling-elephant's trailer; we split
honey-ham sandwiches, silverskins,
sip Turkish tea from a vacuum flask.

Miles vanish as we play *I Spy* and *Hang-
the-Man*. Mr Novacek hums *Don't Fence
Me In* and we start to drift, ache for sequin-
spangled canvas skies as blear-eyed kids
from lightless farms queue at ends of lanes
sharing a single fob-watch, watching caged
wildness and parti-coloured caravans roll
down empty roads for another whole year.

Melancholy Baby

The mechanical newcomer never sleeps
through: four onwards he coils
tight on Silver Cross springs
under the birdlessest of branches.

I feel for missed systoles, root
for rug-hooks, labelled jars of panda
eyes at the backs of shelves
in a pantry chaotic with pianoforte
wire, zinc hairpins, chandler's wax.
In his birdless corner my cuckoo
overwinds clockwork trains.

Health visitors stopped filing
months back. Immunisation tick-
boxes incomplete. I elaborate
on toy-museum postcards how
he's gaining weight, is the spit
of an uncle; shock-blue irises.
In snapshots I mean to enclose, the face
tilts anglewise. At days' ends
we listen to ships' visibilities, nervy
of dark corners, gloss fumes.
Saint Geppetto's vigil is marked
and Tinderbox Night.
                        A craft to keep warm,
that raspy night-hack has me awake,
taps tin-tack semaphores through bone.

Take to the Sea

Sit this one out on the westermost promontory.
Track ghost hulks with black rigging
knitted plumb to the skyline. Schedule
the outward for a lifting tide.
Round trip perhaps.
                                    Leave Sunday at dawn:
a partial eclipse augurs. Tap the mercury.
Chart trade winds. Some guesswork.
A north-easterly would be a godsend. Rely
on your eighth sense. Observe estuary
mudlarks for clues.
                                    Give the harbourmaster
your route-map, in case. Some aren't seen
for decades.

A single knapsack with pouches, chrome yellow
oilskins, a dog-eared polaroid from when you
met, blanched almonds for basecamp soirées.

A fall of snowgeese startles you back to Lir's
children, the icy struggle. Slide-show memories:
helter-skelter seafront music, garlands
of coloured bulbs, postcards from your children:
imprints you'll need if it gets to that.
                                    Enough
to see you through twisters, squalls. Allow yourself
a parting phonecall, holler over static on the seabed
cable, make sure you're heard across the Forties.

Auguries

Mother's cousins in floral-print
frocks would catwalk past
billowing winceyettes and cottons
on a taut summer clothesline;
the house thrown open to sheer light,
air fresh with Windolene
and wax polish. Work done
they'd read leaves in the deeps
of rose china: see twins
for my mother's next confinement;
the recovery of a lost miraculous medal;
a stranger in a blue Hillman reversing
at the lane-end on a Thursday, a flame-haired
woman at his side; an airmail
parcel languishing unconsidered
in the heaped corner of a Brooklyn mailroom.

Stewed leaves rinsed
in the sink's whiteness, the future
swirling clockwise and away. When
my father got home, sheets
unpegged, folded, table set
with oatcakes and Branston,
he'd read aloud from a
folded-back *Belfast Telegraph*
things you might imagine could
never happen.
                    And the day's divinings
would wend swimmy dark ways towards
a Stygian torrent, to wide, wide oceans
of evaded hazards and unforetold loves.

To the Lamp Room

The ferryman mentions a sharp drop
later. Troubling lack of cloudcover.
Penultimate week, he says, over
his rhythmic shoulder, before winter-
mooring her. Yes, frost, surely.

We disembark below a line of
overbright prefabs – petrol-blue,
lilac or cherry – where whin and
scrubby tamarisk shield porches.
Bleachy rose-print curtains expose
Belfast sinks, enamel basins,
cups. No letterboxes. The postvan rarely
slows for such mercy-of-the-tide outposts.
A window shelf displays a late
Clarice Cliff creamer. You pose
for a throwaway camera.
                                          We've regained
our summertime hour today. On our
own this time. We climb ninety-eight
stone treads to the latticed lamp room.
Pineapple-size bulbs, in use the year
my grandfather changed sides.
I scan recessive coastlines, nine yards
gone on a single night once. On the ferry
again the tide has changed. Light
seeps bleakly. Edges of first frost
taste the air. Two kittiwakes stand sentry
by the car wheels. The forecast gives
trouble further out. Trouble, surely.

Before Clock Time

I freeze all timepieces on a Monday
track days by *oscuro* and an eastward
chiaro, as women generations back
on family land would have done
in October, gathering for the dark.
I close curtains early that first
afternoon, read, after a forty-year
gap, *Seal Morning* by Rowena Farre
inscribed *Annie, Thorpeness, '57.*
Isolation deepens.
                I feel already
the thirst (my father's legacy)
for news on the hour. I ponder
on lightkeepers' wives, on death-row
men, on the blind who keep watch
in unlighted rooms. And in another
country, security alarms, fire sirens
sound. Vanilla sponges rise and rise;
babies arrive too soon; ageing lovers
utter last words. Vancouver's buses
run no earlier or later than published.
In Oxford Street Spanish teenagers
queue for roasted chestnuts. And the
leaves beyond my window descend
at fluttering, diastolic intervals
more hushed in light's absence
after capitulation – and sleep – in
timeless night, in a week without time.

Acknowledgements

Acknowledgements are due to the editors of the following publications in which some of these poems first appeared: *Cimarron Review, The Shop, Poetry Wales, Magma, Smiths Knoll, The Interpreter's House, Ulster Tatler, Poetry Review, Fortnight, Acumen, Pitshanger Poets Anthology 2004, Metre, The Rialto, The Independent, London Magazine, Poetry Ireland Review, Poetry Durham, Tears in the Fence, Poetry London, Seam, Fire, Other Poetry, Southfield, Gairfish, The Wolf, Times Literary Supplement* and *The Spectator.*

'Full Dress Rehearsal' appeared in *Ware Poets Anthology* (2010); 'Short Strand' was written for *From the Small Back Room: A Festschrift for Ciaran Carson* (2008); 'Curaçao Dusk' won first prize in the Academi Cardiff International Poetry Competition (2004); 'Novgorod Sidings' was commended in the National Poetry Competition (2003); 'Cirque des Illusions' was commended in the Arvon International Poetry Competition (2002); 'Winterwood' and '6, Sloop Lane' appeared in *The Tabla Book of New Verse* (2001); 'Afternoon on Central Plains Avenue' appeared in *Peterloo Poets: Poetry Competition Anthology* (2000); 'Morning on Bridge Street' appeared in *The Bridport Prize Anthology* (2000); 'Wrong Side of the Moon' appeared in *Peterloo Poets: Poetry Competition Anthology* (1999).

Poems from *The Ghost Twin*, appear courtesy of Peterloo Press, where they were first published in 2005.

Thanks are due to Rockingham Press for permission to include poems from *Late Crossing* (1999) and *Tickets from a Blank Window* (2002).